modern
dim sum

modern
dim sum

Delicious bite-size dumplings, rolls, buns and other small snacks

Loretta Liu

photography by Louise Hagger

RYLAND PETERS & SMALL

LONDON • NEW YORK

Dedication

For Granny, who started my interest in cooking

Senior Designer Sonya Nathoo
Editor Alice Sambrook
Production Manager Gordana Simakovic
Art Director Leslie Harrington
Editorial Director Julia Charles
Publisher Cindy Richards

Food Stylist Emily Kydd
Prop Stylist Jennifer Kay
Recipe Tester Cathy Seward
Indexer Vanessa Bird

First published in 2016 by Ryland Peters & Small
20–21 Jockey's Fields
London WC1R 4BW
and
341 E 116th St,
New York, NY 10029
www.rylandpeters.com

10 9 8 7 6 5 4 3 2 1

Text © Loretta Liu 2016
Design and photographs
© Ryland Peters & Small 2016

ISBN: 978-1-84975-708-9

Printed in China

A CIP record for this book is available from the
British Library. US Library of Congress cataloging-
in-publication data has been applied for.

Notes:

• Both British (Metric) and American (Imperial
plus US cups) measurements are included in these
recipes for your convenience; however, it is
important to work with one set of measurements
and not alternate between the two within a recipe.
• All spoon measurements are level unless otherwise
specified.
• All eggs are medium (UK) or large (US), unless
specified as large, in which case US extra-large
should be used. Uncooked or partially cooked eggs
should not be served to the very old, frail, young
children, pregnant women or those with
compromised immune systems.
• Ovens should be preheated to the specified
temperatures. We recommend using an oven
thermometer. If using a fan-assisted oven, adjust
temperatures according to the manufacturer's
instructions.
• When a recipe calls for the grated zest of citrus fruit,
buy unwaxed fruit and wash well before using. If you
can only find treated fruit, scrub well in warm soapy
water before using.

Author's Acknowledgements

I was brought up by my Granny (now 85 and still
going strong) and grew up listening to wonderful
stories about her childhood and the food she loves.
Originally from China and the daughter of a
magistrate, she had a privileged upbringing and was
exposed to high-end Chinese cuisine. At the age of
16, she married my Grandad and moved to Malaysia,
which offered new and exciting foods to try and cook
for her family. From Granny, I learned how to make
amazing pickles, cook with fresh tofu, whip up a great
curry and prepare dumplings from scratch. It is my
privilege to pass on her authentic cooking lessons to
you the reader. I am very grateful to be given the
chance to write this book, thank you to Julia and my
former editor Kate for commissioning the work. Thank
you to all the team at RPS for making this book
possible. Lastly, thanks to my husband Bing and son
John for the extremely critical job of taste testing.

Contents

Introduction

Dim sum can be loosely translated as 'touch the heart'. It is no wonder that most people get hooked from the very first dumpling. There is nothing quite like the unique dining experience that awaits: an array of intricately made, wonderfully presented little treats. Some are light and healthy, others are golden and crispy. All are meant to be admired and enjoyed among friends. Dim sum chefs are usually highly trained masters of their art. In Chinese culture, the benchmark of a good chef is the quality of their crystal skin dough. The recipe and method are often such closely guarded secrets that they will only be passed down to a single chosen family member!

In this book I reveal how you can make some of the best-loved dim sum dishes in the comfort of your own kitchen. As well as traditional bites I have created modern recipes using flavours inspired by my multicultural upbringing and culinary training. Spanish sundried tomato and olive, Thai red curry, French duck confit, Mongolian lamb, even a creamy British chicken soup from my childhood. The flavour fusions that can be produced are exciting and delicious. Master the basic dough recipes yourself and get creative swapping fillings with folds. I've included tips for achieving professional quality dim sum, the most useful being make a big batch of filling to have with rice or noodles, then use the leftovers to whip up some dumplings the next day. Any of the more unusual ingredients in this book such as Chinese chives or stir-fry sauce can be found in Asian shops/stores or online. Asian white wheat flour achieves the best results for all skins. This is because it has a high gluten content to create the correct texture and a striking pure white colour.

The two dining rituals of tea drinking and dim sum are closely connected and tea plays an important part in the dim sum tradition. Travelling traders on the Silk Road (the world's oldest and most historically important trade route) would stop to drink tea or 'yum cha' and to rest their weary feet. Some teas, such as Oolong or 'blue' tea, work well with most dishes, and regular tea drinkers often have their favourites that they order with every meal. Other more exotic teas have a specific flavour that works better partnered with particular things. A very general rule to follow is the darker the tea, the stronger the flavours it can handle. Hence an earthy black tea is good paired with salty, meaty, spicy or very sweet baked goods. Fresh and grassy green teas are perfect for fried foods like wontons because the flavour cuts through the oil. Delicate white teas are recommended for poultry or vegetarian dishes. Floral teas such Jasmine, Chrysanthemum or Rosebud are light and sweet options that are great with steamed seafood or to cleanse and refresh the palate. Ultimately there is no right or wrong choice when it comes to pairings. Experiment with different teas to find combinations that suit your taste. Whatever your choice, I hope you enjoy the dim sum experience as much as I do.

Basic dough recipes

Wheat dough

150 g/1 cup + 2 tablespooons Asian white wheat flour
80 ml/scant ⅓ cup water
MAKES 16 SKINS

Place the flour in a large mixing bowl and combine with the water to form a dough. Turn the dough out onto a lightly floured surface and knead for 20–25 minutes or until the dough is smooth and elastic. Separate and roll into two equal cylinders about 2.5 cm/ 1 inch in diameter. Cover with a damp kitchen cloth and set aside to rest for 30 minutes.

To prepare the skins, use a sharp knife to slice the dough cylinders into 16 equal pieces. On a lightly floured surface, flatten each piece with a rolling pin until it has a round shape and a diameter of around 7.5 cm/3 inches.

Egg dough

150 g/1 cup plus 2 tablespoons Asian white wheat flour
40 ml/3 tablespoons water
1 egg
MAKES 16 SKINS

Place the flour in a large mixing bowl and add the water and egg. Bring together, then turn the dough out onto a lightly floured surface. Using lightly floured hands, knead for 20–25 minutes. The dough will be sticky at first but should become smooth and silky. Separate in half and roll into two equal cylinders, about 2.5 cm/1 inch in diameter. Cover with a damp kitchen cloth to prevent from drying out and set aside to rest for 30 minutes.

To prepare the skins, use a sharp knife to slice the dough cylinders into 16 equal pieces. On a lightly floured surface, flatten each piece with a rolling pin until it has a round shape and a diameter of around 7.5 cm/3 inches.

Puff pastry dough

Water dough:
100 g/¾ cup Asian white wheat flour
15 g/1 heaped tablespoon caster/superfine sugar
40 ml/3 tablespoons water
30 g/2 tablespoons unsalted butter, melted
Butter dough:
100 g/¾ cup Asian white wheat flour
50 g/3½ tablespoons unsalted butter, melted
MAKES 12 SKINS

In a large mixing bowl, combine the ingredients for the water dough. Form the dough into a ball and knead lightly until smooth and silky. Wrap the dough with clingfilm/plastic wrap and rest in the fridge for 15 minutes. Divide the dough into 12 and roll each piece into a ball. Cover with a damp kitchen cloth and set aside. In a second mixing bowl, repeat the same full process with the butter dough ingredients but instead of chilling, rest at room temperature for 15 minutes.

To assemble the dough, take a water dough ball and knead gently and briefly. Very lightly flour the worktop and use a rolling pin to roll out the ball of water dough to a diameter of 7.5 cm/3 inches. Place a butter dough ball in the centre and wrap the water dough around to enclose it completely. Turn the dough ball over so the join is on the underside. Roll the combined dough into a thick square parcel. Fold the parcel into three and flatten with the rolling pin again. Repeat this fold and roll process twice with each ball. Cover and rest in the fridge for 15 minutes before rolling into the desired shape for the recipe.

Bread dough

2 teaspoons dry easy-bake yeast
450 g/3½ cups Asian white wheat flour
100 g/¾ cup plus 1 tablespoon icing sugar/
   confectioners' sugar, sifted
15 g/2 tablespoons dried milk powder
¼ teaspoon fine salt
2 teaspoons baking powder
180 ml/¾ cup water, add more if needed
50 ml/scant ¼ cup vegetable oil, plus extra
   for oiling the bowl
MAKES 16 SKINS

Place the yeast in a large mixing bowl, then add the flour, sugar, milk powder, salt and baking powder. Make sure the yeast is separated from the salt by the layer of flour. Add the water and oil and bring together with a dough scraper. When no dry flour remains, remove the dough from the bowl and place on a lightly floured surface. Knead firmly for 5–10 minutes, until smooth and elastic.

Lightly oil the mixing bowl. Shape the dough into two cylinders and place back in the oiled bowl, cover with oiled clingfilm/plastic wrap and leave in a warm place to rise for 40–60 minutes or until doubled in size.

Remove the risen dough from the bowl, punch it down and knead it again briefly, but very carefully rather than firmly this time. Roll the dough out into a big rectangle and portion it out into 16 equal balls. Cover the dough balls with oiled clingfilm/plastic wrap and leave to rest again for 30 minutes in a warm place.

Roll out each dough ball so that it has a diameter of around 7.5 cm/3 inches; try to make the centre slightly thicker than the edges so that it can hold the filling. Cover each dough circle with a damp kitchen cloth as you finish to stop it from drying out.

Crystal skin dough

100 g/¾ cup wheat starch
50 g/½ cup tapioca starch
a pinch of fine salt
150 ml/⅔ cup boiling (not hot) water
MAKES 16 SKINS

In a large mixing bowl, combine the wheat starch, tapioca starch and salt. Add the boiling water and mix with a wooden spoon until a dough is formed. Transfer to a lightly floured surface and knead until smooth. Separate the dough in half and roll into two equal cylinders, about 2.5 cm/1 inch in diameter. Wrap in clingfilm/plastic wrap and rest until needed.

Divide the dough into 16 equal balls. On a lightly floured surface use a rolling pin to flatten the dough balls into thin discs, about 5 cm/2 inches in diameter. Cover the finished skins with a damp kitchen cloth as you work so that they don't dry out.

Meat

Traditional jiaozi are extremely popular at holiday celebrations such as Chinese New Year. Often prepared in an assembly line by various family members, these tasty dumplings are enjoyed by children and adults alike. The folded, plump pleated shape is a nice easy one to start with.

Pork and leek jiaozi

1 batch Wheat Dough, page 8
100 g/3½ oz. firm tofu, drained and sliced into small cubes
a pinch of salt
100 g/3½ oz. minced/ground pork
2 Chinese chive stalks, white parts removed, finely chopped
a large handful of fresh coriander/cilantro, chopped
1 teaspoon Sichuan pepper
1 teaspoon black pepper
2 tablespons dark soy sauce
2 tablespoons sesame oil
1 leek, finely chopped
2 button mushrooms, finely chopped
1 tablespoon sunflower oil
black vinegar, for dipping

MAKES 16

Prepare the wheat dough following the instructions from the basic recipe on page 8. While the dough is resting, begin the filling. Sprinkle the tofu slices with salt and set aside for 30 minutes before squeezing out the excess water.

In a large bowl mix the minced/ground pork with the tofu and the rest of the ingredients apart from the sunflower oil and black vinegar.

Roll out the skins, continuing to follow the instructions from the recipe on page 8. Place a small tablespoon of filling neatly into the centre of a skin. Dip your fingertips into a small dish of water and slightly moisten the edge of half the skin. Fold the skin in half over the filling. Pinch one end together and make small folds to form pleats. The end result should be a plump sealed pocket.

Tap the dumplings base-down on your work surface to finish. As you are working, set aside the finished dumplings on a floured baking sheet under a damp cloth so they do not dry out.

Heat the sunflower oil over a medium heat in a large frying pan/skillet. Lightly fry the dumplings until golden brown on the bottom. To finish off the cooking process, place the dumplings in a large pan of boiling water. Cover with a lid and poach until they float to the surface.

Serve the dumplings hot with black vinegar for dipping.

Pork and cabbage are a popular choice of filling for home cooks in China because they are protein-packed yet inexpensive ingredients. But that doesn't stop these dumplings from being ridiculously tempting. Create the flower shape by lightly squeezing the egg dough cup in the middle.

Pork and cabbage shumai

1 batch Egg Dough, page 8
100 g/3½ oz. raw prawns/shrimp, peeled and deveined
100 g/3½ oz. lean minced/ ground pork
60 g/1¼ cups chopped cabbage
1 tablespoon oyster sauce
½ tablespoon sesame oil
1 teaspoon freshly ground white pepper
1 tablespoon cornflour/cornstarch
1 teaspoon salt
toasted white sesame seeds, to garnish

Dipping sauce
125 ml/½ cup soy sauce
2 tablespoons sesame oil
a large handful of fresh coriander/cilantro, chopped
2 spring onions/scallions, sliced
1 teaspoon crushed/minced garlic
1 tablespoon grated fresh ginger

a bamboo steamer, lined with parchment paper

MAKES 16

Prepare the egg dough following the instructions from the basic recipe on page 8. While the dough is resting, make the filling. Mince the prawns/shrimp using a sharp knife to finely chop into small pieces. Transfer to a large mixing bowl, add the rest of the filling ingredients and mix thoroughly.

Roll out the egg dough, continuing to follow the instructions from the recipe on page 8. To assemble the shumai, place a wrapper on your palm and add a small tablespoon of filling to the centre. Gather the edges of the wrapper and gently pleat so that a basket shape is formed up and around the filling, leaving the middle exposed. Lightly tap the base of the dumpling on a countertop to flatten the bottom and make sure the filling fills the nooks and crannies. Lightly squeeze the middle with your thumb and forefinger to create the classic flower shape. Repeat for the rest of the wrappers and filling.

Arrange the shumai at the bottom of the lined bamboo steamer, leaving plenty of space between each one. Cover and steam the dumplings over boiling water for 7 minutes or until cooked through.

Make the dipping sauce while the dumplings are steaming by stirring the ingredients together in a small bowl.

Remove the dumplings from the steamer using the parchment paper to assist. Serve warm sprinkled with toasted white sesame seeds and alongside the dipping sauce.

The pillowy-soft bread bun surrounding sweet and sticky char siu-style pork is just a heavenly combination. Traditionally, the filling for this type of dumpling used up leftovers from dinner the night before.

Barbecue pork bao

1 batch Bread Dough, page 9
1 tablespoon sunflower oil
1 shallot, chopped
2 tablespoons dry sherry
350 g/12 oz. pork loin, diced
1 teaspoon crushed/minced garlic
2 tablespoons honey
2 tablespoons hoisin sauce
1 teaspoon Chinese five-spice powder
1 tablespoon soy sauce

a bamboo steamer, lined with parchment paper

MAKES 16

To make the filling, heat the oil in a flameproof casserole dish and add the shallot. Cook over a medium heat until softened and lightly caramelized, about 5–7 minutes. Pour in the sherry and let the alcohol cook out for a few minutes. Lower the heat a little and add the pork. Cook, stirring, for a further 2 minutes or until lightly browned.

Meanwhile, in a separate bowl mix the garlic, honey, hoisin sauce, Chinese five-spice powder and soy sauce with 2 tablespoons of water. Add this to the pork and shallot mixture. Stir well. Cover and cook over a low heat for 1 hour or until the sauce has thickened and the pork is tender. Check occasionally during cooking to ensure the sauce does not dry out. Add a little extra water if necessary.

While the pork is cooking, prepare the bread dough following the instructions from the basic recipe on page 9. While the dough is rising, allow the pork mixture to cool and finely chop the meat.

Continue to follow the instructions from the bread dough recipe on page 9. Once the skins are ready, place 1 heaped tablespoon of the filling in the centre of each round. Gather the edges to form pleats and pinch to seal the top of the bun.

Set the finished buns into the lined bamboo steamer at least 5 cm/ 2 inches apart. You may have to do this in batches depending on the size of your steamer.

Cover with oiled clingfilm/plastic wrap and allow to rise for a last 30 minutes. Steam over boiling water for 8–10 minutes until the dough is light and fluffy. Cool the buns slightly and serve.

Light flaky pastry is here the yin to the yang of the dark and rich barbecue pork. The Chinese way of making puff pastry using combined butter dough and water dough originates from Hong Kong, and it's a little healthier than the Western way of packing in as much butter as possible.

Barbecue pork puff

1 batch Puff Pastry Dough, page 8
1 tablespoon sunflower oil
1 shallot, chopped
2 tablespoons dry sherry
225 g/8 oz. pork loin, diced
1 teaspoon crushed/minced garlic
2 tablespoons honey
2 tablespoons hoisin sauce
1 teaspoon Chinese five-spice
  powder
1 tablespoon soy sauce
1 egg, beaten
black sesame seeds, to garnish

a large baking sheet, greased

MAKES 12

For the filling, heat the oil a flameproof casserole dish and add the chopped shallot. Cook until softened and lightly caramelized, about 5–7 minutes. Pour in the sherry and let the alcohol cook out. Lower the heat to medium and add in the diced pork. Cook, stirring, for an extra 2 minutes or until lightly browned.

Meanwhile, mix the garlic, honey, hoisin sauce, five-spice powder and soy sauce in a bowl with 2 tablespoons of water. Add this to the pork and shallot, stirring well. Cover and cook for 1 hour over a low heat until the sauce has thickened and the pork is soft. Check occasionally during cooking to ensure the sauce does not dry out. Add a little extra water if necessary.

While the pork is cooking, prepare the puff pastry dough balls following the instructions from the basic recipe on page 8. Chill in the fridge until needed.

Preheat the oven to 200°C/400°F/Gas 6. Finely chop the pork once it is cool, ready for filling the pastry.

Roll each pastry ball into a rectangle 10 x 6 cm/4 x 2½ inches and then cut each in half widthways. Put a small tablespoon of filling on one half, brush the edges with beaten egg and position the second piece of pastry on top. Use a fork to make indentations and to tightly seal the edges.

Place the parcels on the greased baking sheet, brush the tops with beaten egg and sprinkle with black sesame seeds to garnish. Bake in the preheated oven for 20–25 minutes or until golden brown. Serve warm.

Translating literally as 'fire meat' in Korean, beef bulgogi is a flavoursome dish of marinated grilled beef. The recipe was introduced to China by the migrant population of Korea. Using a good cut of beef here is key; you want the meat to be almost as soft as the flaky pastry on the outside.

Beef bulgogi puffs

1 batch Puff Pastry Dough, page 8
4 spring onions/scallions finely chopped
½ onion, finely chopped
¼ pineapple (pear or kiwi will also work), finely chopped
1 tablespoon dark soy sauce
1 tablespoon sugar
1 teaspoon sesame oil
freshly ground black pepper
2 garlic cloves, crushed/minced
1 tablespoon freshly squeezed lemon juice
150 g/5¼ oz. sirloin steak, sliced into bite-size strips
1 egg, beaten
white sesame seeds, to garnish
chilli/chile sauce, for dipping

a griddle/grill pan, lightly greased
a large baking sheet, greased

MAKES 12

Stir together the filling ingredients, apart from the meat, in a large bowl to form a marinade paste, adding a little water to loosen if necessary.

Mix the beef strips with the paste, making sure that each strip is well coated. Leave in the fridge to marinate for at least 30 minutes and up to 2 hours, left longer than this the beef may become too salty.

While the meat is marinating, prepare the 12 puff pastry dough balls following the instructions in the basic recipe on page 8. Chill in the fridge until needed.

Heat a griddle/grill pan over a medium-high heat, add the beef strips and juices to the pan and cook to until the meat is browned around the edges and cooked to your liking, around 3–7 minutes. Remove from the pan and leave to cool.

Preheat the oven to 200°C/400°F/Gas 6.

Roll each pastry ball into a square about 10 cm/4 inches along each edge. Put a tablespoon of filling in the middle and brush the edges with a little beaten egg. Fold the pastry in half diagonally to create a triangle. Seal the edges then tuck the seams underneath to create a smooth finish on top. Repeat with the remaining dough and filling.

Place the puffs on the greased baking sheet, brush with beaten egg, sprinkle with sesame seeds and bake for 20–25 minutes until golden brown. Serve with chilli/chile sauce for dipping.

Slow-cooked pork flavoured with five-spice and paired with the savoury tang of olives is a modern take on an Asian classic that works so well.

Pulled pork and olive dumplings

1 batch Crystal Skin Dough, page 9

1-kg/2-lbs. shoulder of pork from the neck-end, bone in (once cooked with bone and fat removed this should equate to roughly 250 g/9 oz. meat)

1 tablespoon salt

1 tablespoon dark muscovado sugar

2 teaspoons Chinese five-spice powder

35 g/⅓ cup of black pitted olives, chopped

a roasting pan big enough for a shoulder of pork, lined with foil

a bamboo steamer, lined with parchment paper

MAKES 16

Preheat the oven to 220°C/425°F/Gas 7.

Place the pork shoulder in the foil-lined roasting pan and pat the meat dry with paper towels. Mix the dry ingredients together and rub into the pork. Wrap the shoulder in the foil, making sure that it is fully enclosed.

Place the pork in the preheated oven. After 40 minutes, turn the heat down to 125°C/250°F/Gas½ and cook for a further 4–6 hours until the pork is very tender. (Check occasionally during cooking time that the pork is not drying out; add a little water if it is.)

While the filling is cooking, prepare the crystal skin dough following the instructions from the basic recipe on page 9. Rest wrapped in clingfilm/plastic wrap until needed.

Once the meat has cooked, unwrap the joint, strain and set aside the juices. Remove the bone and fat from the meat and discard. Use a fork to pull the pork into shreds. Mix the chopped olives into the pulled pork and set aside to cool.

When the filling has cooled, roll out the skins. Place a large teaspoon of filling into the centre of each skin and gather the edges with your fingertips to make a round dumpling shape. Make small folds all the way around the top edge to create pleats. Pleat all the way around until the filling is enclosed.

Place the dumplings in the lined bamboo steamer over a high heat and steam for 15–20 minutes or until transparent. Just before serving warm the pulled pork juices for dipping.

Sheep are a plentiful cattle high up in the cold mountains of Mongolia, hence this speciality dish. With their strong, savoury flavour, these are delicious eaten steaming hot on a chilly day.

Mongolian lamb and mint dumplings

1 batch Wheat Dough, page 8
100 g/3½ oz. firm tofu, drained and sliced into small cubes
a pinch of salt
2 tablespoons rapeseed/canola oil
1 red onion, cubed
1 teaspoon cumin seeds
1 teaspoon coriander seeds
⅓ small head Chinese cabbage
200 g/7 oz. minced/ground lamb
2 Chinese chive stalks, white parts removed, finely chopped
a large handful of fresh mint leaves, shredded
1 spring onion/scallion, finely chopped
1 teaspoon minced fresh ginger
2 tablespoons soy sauce
1 tablespoon sunflower oil

Dipping sauce
a handful of fresh mint leaves, finely shredded
2 tablespoons sesame oil
1 small red shallot, finely chopped
1 fresh chilli/chile, finely chopped
3 tablespoons soy sauce

MAKES 16

Prepare the wheat dough following the instructions in the basic recipe on page 8. While the dough is resting, prepare the filling. Sprinkle salt over the tofu slices and set them aside for 30 minutes before squeezing out the excess water.

Place the rapeseed/canola oil and cubed onion in a small frying pan/skillet and cook over a medium heat until soft and translucent. Add the cumin and coriander seeds and fry until fragrant. Transfer to a large mixing bowl to let cool.

Remove any tough stalks from the cabbage and boil the leaves until soft. Drain well and wrap in a clean, dry kitchen cloth to remove any excess moisture. Finely shred the dry leaves and add to the onions in the mixing bowl. Add the lamb, herbs, spring onion/scallion, ginger, soy sauce and tofu and and mix to combine.

Roll out the dough following the instructions on page 8. Place a large teaspoon of filling into the centre of each skin. Dip your fingertips in a small dish of water and slightly moisten the edge of half the skin. Fold the skin in half over the filling, and pinch the corners together to shape into a traditional half-moon crescent. Add a few little folded pleats along the edge as you seal.

Put a pan of water on to boil and gently lower the dumplings into the boiling water. Cover with a lid. The dumplings are cooked when they float to the top.

Drain the dumplings and let them cool slightly. For the dipping sauce, mix the ingredients together in a small bowl and set aside. Pan-fry the dumplings in the sunflower oil over a medium heat until lightly brown and crisp at the base. Drain on paper towels and serve immediately with the dipping sauce.

Poultry

Inspired by my classic French culinary training, juicy duck confit with the flavour of aromatic crispy duck is a delectable treat.

Duck confit puff

1 batch Puff Pastry Dough, page 8

2 duck legs

60 g/¼ cup sea salt flakes, plus extra for serving

1 tablespoon freshly ground black pepper

1 garlic clove, crushed/minced

2 tablespoons Chinese five-spice powder

5 star anise

1 cinnamon stick

2 cloves

500 g/1 lb. duck fat

2 spring onions/scallions, chopped

2 tablespoons hoisin sauce

1 egg, beaten

white sesame seeds, to garnish

a small round pastry cutter

MAKES 12

Rub the duck legs with the sea salt flakes, black pepper, crushed/minced garlic clove, five-spice powder, star anise, cinnamon stick and cloves. Pack the duck and these ingredients tightly into a dish, skin-side down. Cover the dish with clingfilm/ plastic wrap and leave to marinate in the fridge for 24 hours.

Preheat the oven to 150°C/300°F/Gas 2.

Scrape the marinade off the duck pieces. Heat the duck fat in an ovenproof dish until melted, then add the duck legs, ensuring they are completely submerged.

Bake the duck in the preheated oven for 3½ hours, or until the meat is very tender when pierced with a skewer and the fat in the skin is rendered. Once cooked, remove the duck from the fat and allow to cool uncovered. Shred finely and mix with the chopped spring onions/scallions and hoisin sauce.

Prepare and roll out the puff pastry dough following the instructions from the basic recipe on page 8. Using a small round pastry cutter, stamp out 2 rounds from each dough ball portion. Put a spoonful of filling on one half, brush the edges with beaten egg and position the second piece of pastry on top. Use a fork to make indentations around the edge to tightly seal.

Brush the tops with beaten egg and sprinkle with white sesame seeds. Bake in the preheated oven for 20–25 minutes until golden brown.

These tasty morsels commemorate my love of Campbell's canned chicken soup as a child. The mild flavours mean that these dumplings would be a great way of introducing young children to dim sum.

Chicken and potato cream stew dumpling

1 batch Crystal Skin Dough, page 9
2 tablespoons unsalted butter
½ medium onion, finely chopped
½ medium carrot, finely diced
½ celery stalk, finely diced
1 medium potato, peeled and finely diced
1 tablespoon plain/all-purpose flour
1 chicken stock cube
175 ml/¾ cup milk
1 chicken breast, finely diced
½ teaspoon each salt and freshly ground black pepper
melted butter, for dipping

a bamboo steamer, lined with parchment paper

MAKES 16

Prepare the crystal skin dough following the intructions from the basic recipe on page 9. Wrap in clingfilm/plastic wrap and rest until needed.

Melt the butter in a large pan over a medium heat. Add the diced onion, carrot, celery and potato. Cook, stirring occasionally, until tender, about 3–4 minutes.

Whisk in the flour slowly and heat for a minute. Next crumble the stock cube into the pan and gradually add the milk, whisking constantly. Continue cooking and stirring until the sauce has slightly thickened, about 1–2 minutes.

Add the chicken. Bring the sauce to a boil; reduce heat and simmer until the potatoes and chicken are tender, about 12–15 minutes. Set aside to cool.

While the filling is cooling, roll out the crystal skin dough following the intructions on page 9. Place a large teaspoon of filling into the centre of each skin. Fold the dumplings in half and pinch the edges together to form a simple crescent shape.

Space out the dumplings evenly in the bamboo steamer lined with parchment paper. Steam over boiling water for 15–20 minutes or until the skins turn transparent. Serve warm with the hot melted butter for dipping.

A simple and delicious favourite served with a garlic, ginger and chilli/chile oil. These are the classic flavours of Asia. The amount of hot pepper powder can be added more or less to taste.

Spicy chicken and shrimp dumplings

1 batch Wheat Dough, page 8
1 chicken breast
60 g/2¼ oz. raw prawns/shrimp, peeled and deveined
1 leek, chopped
2 Chinese chive stalks, chopped
a large handful of fresh coriander/cilantro, chopped
½–1 tablespoon Korean hot pepper powder (to taste)
1 teaspoon freshly ground black pepper
1 tablespoon oyster sauce
½ tablespoon sesame oil

Dipping sauce
1 garlic clove, finely chopped
1 tablespoon grated fresh ginger
6 tablespoons soy sauce
2 tablespoons chilli/chile oil

MAKES 16

Prepare the wheat dough following the instructions in the basic recipe on page 8, and rest wrapped in clingfilm/plastic wrap until needed. Meanwhile, mince the chicken breast and prawns/shrimp using a sharp knife to very finely chop. Transfer to a mixing bowl and combine with the rest of the filling ingredients. Chill in the fridge for 30 minutes.

Roll out the skins, continuing to follow the basic recipe on page 8. Put a large teaspoon of filling into the centre of each skin. Dip your fingertips in a small dish of water and slightly moisten the edge of half the skin. Seal the dumpling up tightly using your fingers to pinch, pull and fold the skin into 4 pleats at the join. Repeat the process until all the mixture and skins have been used.

Bring a large pan of water to boiling point. Gently lower in the dumplings and cover with a lid to poach. The dumplings are cooked when they float to the top of the liquid.

To make the dipping sauce, mix together all the ingredients. Drain the dumplings and serve at once accompanied with the dipping sauce.

If you prefer a crispy base, you can lightly pan-fry the uncooked dumplings in a small amount of oil and finish off the cooking by poaching in water or stock (see instructions on page 11).

A taste of Thailand fused with traditional Chinese bao (or baozi to give them their full name) in these beautiful red curry buns.

Red curry chicken and lentil bao

1 batch Bread Dough, page 9

2 tablespoons sunflower oil

2 onions, finely sliced

2 garlic cloves, crushed/minced

1–2 tablespoons Thai red curry
   paste (to taste)

2 chicken breasts, cut into
   bite-size pieces

500 ml/2 cups hot chicken stock

80 g/scant ½ cup dried red lentils

*a bamboo steamer, lined with
   parchment paper*

MAKES 16

Make the bread dough following the instructions in the basic recipe on page 9. While the dough is rising, prepare the filling.

Heat 1 tablespoon of the oil in a large frying pan/skillet and add the onions. Cook for 3 minutes over a gentle heat until soft and fragrant. Stir in the crushed/minced garlic and curry paste and cook for 1–2 minutes more.

Add the chicken pieces and cook for 2–3 minutes. Stir in the stock and lentils, bring to the boil, cover and simmer for 25 minutes, stirring occasionally, until the lentils are tender and the chicken is cooked. Set aside to cool.

Continue to follow the instructions from the bread dough recipe on page 9. Once the skins are ready, place 1 tablespoon of the filling in the centre of each round. Gather and pleat the edges, pinching to seal the top of the bun.

Set the finished buns in the lined bamboo steamer about 5 cm/2 inches apart. You may have to do this in batches depending on the size of your steamer. Cover with oiled clingfilm/plastic wrap and allow to rise for another 30 minutes.

Once risen, steam the bao over a high heat for 15–20 minutes or until the dough is light and fluffy. Cool slightly and serve.

The lotus is considered a sacred plant in Chinese culture, the fruit of which is delicious but hard to find. More prevalent are the giant strong-textured leaves, perfect for holding filling but still pleasant to eat.

Lotus leaf rice dumplings

370 g/2 cups sweet glutinous/
  sticky rice
4 dried lotus leaves
½ teaspoon salt
1 teaspoon sesame oil
1 chicken breast, finely chopped
1 tablespoon cornflour/cornstarch
2 teaspoons vegetable oil
4 shiitake mushrooms, sliced
1 leek, sliced
1 Chinese sausage (marinated and
  smoked pork sausage found in
  Chinese markets), thinly sliced
2 teaspoons oyster sauce
2 teaspoons soy sauce
1 tablespoon Shaoxing rice wine
2 tablespoons caster/superfine
  sugar

*a bamboo steamer, lined with
  parchment paper*
a rice cooker

MAKES 8

Rinse and drain the rice, then soak in 600 ml/2½ cups water for 2 hours.

Meanwhile, cut each folded lotus leaf in half lengthways. Submerge the leaves in hot water and leave to soak for 30 minutes, pressing down if they float up. Trim the leaves with kitchen scissors/shears until they are a similar size and trim off the hard stalk end.

Drain the rice thoroughly. In the bowl of a rice cooker, place the rice, salt, sesame oil and 250 ml/1 cup water. Cook following the packet instructions.

Mix the chopped chicken with the cornflour/cornstarch. Put the oil in a large frying pan/skillet over a high heat and fry the chicken for 3 minutes. Add the mushrooms, sliced leek and sausage and cook, stirring for a further few minutes. Lower the heat and add the oyster sauce, soy sauce, Shaoxing rice wine and caster/superfine sugar. Stir-fry until chicken is cooked and the vegetables are tender. Set aside to cool.

Divide the cooked rice into 8 portions. With wet fingertips, divide each portion of rice in half. Shape 8 half-portions into rectangles in the centre of each lotus leaf half. Put 1 tablespoon of chicken mixture on top and spread evenly. Top the meat with the other halves of rice to cover them completely.

Fold the bottom of the leaves up over the rice. Fold in the left and right sides, and then roll each leaf away from you towards the curved edge to make a rectangular packet. Place the dumplings seam-side down on the bamboo steamer. Steam over boiling water for 45 minutes, or until heated through. Serve warm.

Fish and seafood

Also known as har gao, these little dumplings are one of the most iconic dim sum dishes. The crystal skin should be delicate enough to just about see the pink shrimp peeping through.

Traditional shrimp dumplings

1 batch Crystal Skin Dough, page 9
50 g/1¾ oz. firm tofu, drained and sliced
150 g/5¼ oz. raw prawns/ shrimp, peeled and deveined
1 teaspoon minced fresh ginger
1 teaspoon crushed/minced garlic
½ teaspoon Shaoxing rice wine
½ teaspoon salt
½ teaspoon sugar
½ teaspoon ground white pepper
1 teaspoon olive oil
1 teaspoon cornflour/cornstarch

Dipping sauce
1 small piece fresh ginger, peeled and finely sliced
6 tablespoons black vinegar

a bamboo steamer lined with parchment paper

MAKES 16

Squeeze out the excess water from the tofu and finely mince using a sharp knife.

Chop each prawn/shrimp into 4–5 small pieces and place in a bowl. Add the drained and minced tofu, ginger, garlic, Shaoxing rice wine, salt, sugar, white pepper, oil, and cornflour/cornstarch. Mix well and set aside in the fridge to marinate while you make the dough.

Prepare, rest and then roll out the crystal skin dough following the instructions in the basic recipe on page 9. Place a large teaspoon of filling neatly into the centre of a skin. Fold the skin in half over the filling. Pinch one end together and start to crimp the edge by making small folds to form pleats to create the traditional crescent shape.

Put the dumplings into the bamboo steamer lined with parchment paper. Steam over boiling water for 15–20 minutes or until the skin is transparent and the prawns/shrimp are red.

To make the dipping sauce, stir the minced ginger into the black vinegar. Serve the dumplings hot alongside the dipping sauce.

The scallop is the pearlescent jewel in the crown of these dumplings, which are great for impressing guests at a dinner party. The spicy lime-based dipping sauce is the perfect complement to the luxurious seafood filling.

Scallop and crab dumplings

1 batch Crystal Skin Dough, page 9
1 leek, finely chopped
60 g/2¼ oz. fresh crab meat, flaked
1 teaspoon minced fresh ginger
1 teaspoon crushed/minced garlic
½ teaspoon salt
½ teaspoon ground white pepper
½ teaspoon Shaoxing rice wine
½ teaspoon sugar
1 teaspoon sesame oil
1 teaspoon cornflour/cornstarch
16 scallops

Dipping sauce
4 tablespoons sugar
2 tablespoons water
2 tablespoons white vinegar
1 garlic clove, crushed/minced
1 tablespoon fish sauce
1 teaspoon Indonesian chilli/chile
   sauce
freshly squeezed juice of 2 limes
a handful of fresh coriander/cilantro,
   finely chopped

*a bamboo steamer lined with
   parchment paper*

MAKES 16

Begin by making the dipping sauce. Boil the sugar, water and vinegar in a small saucepan until the sugar has dissolved. Turn down the heat to medium, stir in the garlic, fish sauce and chilli/chile sauce and simmer for 1 minute. Remove from the heat. Cool and add the lime juice and coriander/cilantro. Set aside ready for later.

Prepare the crystal dough following the instructions in the basic recipe on page 9. While the dough is resting make the filling. In a bowl combine the leek, crab meat, ginger, garlic, seasoning, Shaoxing rice wine, sugar, oil and cornflour/cornstarch; mix well.

Roll out the crystal dough skins, continuing to follow the instructions on page 9. Put a large teaspoon of the crab mixture into the centre of each skin and place a scallop on the top. Fold the skin in half over the filling, and pinch together the sides to create the traditional crescent shaped dumpling. Fold the two ends of the dumpling inwards so that they overlap. Press together to seal and form the Chinese ingot shape.

Place the dumplings into the bamboo steamer lined with parchment paper. Steam over boiling water for 15–20 minutes or until the skin is transparent.

Serve the dumplings hot with the dipping sauce.

These bread buns are intensely delicious yet classy comfort food. With the surprise of a whole scallop in the centre, they are sure to be a winner. Separate dipping sauces are not usually needed with bread buns such as these as the filling inside should be juicy enough.

Fried shrimp and scallop bao

1 batch Bread Dough, page 9
2 spring onions/scallions, chopped
¼ head of cabbage, chopped
400 g/14 oz. raw prawns/shrimp, peeled and deveined
3 tablespoons oyster sauce
2 tablespoons Korean chilli flakes/hot pepper flakes
1 tablespoon sesame oil
2 tablespoons Shaoxing rice wine
16 scallops

a bamboo steamer, lined with parchment paper

MAKES 16

Make the bread dough following the instructions from the basic recipe on page 9, leave to rise while you prepare the filling.

Mix the spring onions/scallions and cabbage together in a large bowl. Mince the prawns/shrimp by chopping them very finely with a sharp knife. Add these to the vegetables along with the oyster sauce, chilli flakes/hot pepper flakes, sesame oil and Shaoxing rice wine. Mix together well and chill in the fridge.

Continue to follow the instructions from the bread dough recipe on page 9. Once the skins are ready, place 1 tablespoon of the prawn/shrimp filling in the centre and a scallop on top. Pull and pleat the edges of the dough to enclose the filling and pinch to seal the tops of the buns.

Set the buns in the lined bamboo steamer about 5 cm/2 inches apart. You may have to do this in batches depending on the size of your steamer. Cover with oiled clingfilm/plastic wrap and let rise for a final 30 minutes.

Steam the buns over boiling water for 8–10 minutes until the dough is light and fluffy. Let cool slightly and serve.

Deep-fried golden crispy wontons are a moreish pleasure to eat. The tropical mango dipping sauce provides a sweet and sharp tang to cut through the savouriness of the skin. Folding in this rustic way is simple to do but the finish is very effective.

Shrimp and mango wontons

350 g/12½ oz. fresh prawns/shrimp, peeled and deveined
1 teaspoons salt
1 teaspoon freshly ground black pepper
a small handful of fresh coriander/cilantro, chopped
50 g/1¾ oz. firm tofu, drained and sliced
1 packet 16 wonton wrappers
sunflower oil, for deep-frying

Dipping sauce
4 tablepoons mayonnaise
2 teaspoons condensed milk
¼ small mango, diced into small cubes

MAKES 16

Use a pestle and mortar to mince the prawns/shrimp to a fine paste. Season with the salt and pepper and mix in the coriander/cilantro. Squeeze any excess water from the tofu, mash with a fork and add to the paste, stir well.

Hold a wonton skin on the palm of your hand and add a heaped teaspoon of filling to the centre. Dab the edges of the skin with a tiny bit of water and gather and scrunch the sides together in a rustic fashion. Repeat until all the filling and skins are used.

Heat the oil in a deep-fryer or large pan until it reaches 180°C/350°F. Cook the wontons in the hot oil in small batches for around a minute on either side. The wontons are cooked when they float up and the skins have turned golden brown. Drain the excess oil on paper towels.

To make dipping sauce, sweeten the mayonnaise with the condensed milk and stir in the diced mango. Serve the wontons hot with the mango dipping sauce.

Salmon is a popular ingredient in any cuisine. It works well with the light texture of a crystal skin dough and the pink against the white is attractive.

Salmon and mushroom dumplings

1 batch Crystal Skin Dough, page 9
1 tablespoon sunflower oil
1 oyster mushroom
1 bunch enoki mushrooms
3 shiitaki mushrooms
20 g/¼ cup chanterelle mushrooms
1 garlic clove, finely chopped
1 small salmon fillet
1 tablespoon minced fresh ginger

1 Chinese chive stalk,
    white parts removed,
chilli/chile oil, to serve

a small round pastry cutter

*a bamboo steamer, lined with
    parchment paper*

MAKES 16

Prepare the crystal skin dough following the basic recipe on page 9, and make the filling while the dough is resting.

Slice the mushrooms into small, even pieces. Heat the sunflower oil in a pan/skillet and fry the mushrooms and garlic over a medium heat until fragrant. Set aside to cool, discarding any excess juice.

Roll out the crystal skin dough and stamp out 24 circles using the small round pastry cutter. Portion the salmon fillet into 12 pieces and cut the Chinese chives into 3-cm/2-inch lengths.

Place a salmon piece in the centre of a skin, add a sprinkle of minced ginger and a chive piece neatly on the top. Lastly, top with a teaspoon of the cooked mushrooms. Cover with another round skin and press around the edge to seal.

Place the dumplings into the lined bamboo steamer and steam over boiling water until transparent. Serve hot with chilli/chile oil.

A best-ever version of a classic, often requested in dim sum restaurants. Here is how to cook this favourite in the comfort of your own home.

Salt and pepper squid

3 fresh whole squid, cleaned
1 tablespoon Shaoxing rice wine
2 tablespoons sesame oil
vegetable oil for deep-frying
100 g/¾ cup plain/all-purpose flour
50 g/⅓ cup semolina
1 teaspoon salt
1 tablespoon freshly ground white pepper
1 tablespoon sunflower oil
2 teaspoons minced fresh ginger
2 garlic cloves, crushed/minced
2 small green chillies/chiles, sliced
2 small red chillies/chiles, sliced
2 curry leaves
salt and freshly ground black pepper, to taste

SERVES 4–5 AS A SMALL DISH

Remove the tentacles from the body of the cleaned squid. Slice the body widthways into 3-cm/1-inch thick strips. Cut the tentacles into 4-cm/1½-inch long pieces.

Place the squid in a bowl with the Shaoxing rice wine and sesame oil. Cover with clingfilm/plastic wrap and leave in the fridge to marinate for 30 minutes.

Heat the oil in a deep-fryer or large pan until it reaches 180°C/350°F.

Mix together the flour, semolina, salt and white pepper in a bowl. Toss the squid in the dry mixture to coat thoroughly.

Using a long-handled sieve/strainer, lower the squid into the hot oil. Deep-fry until golden brown. Drain the cooked squid on paper towels and season to taste with salt and pepper.

Add 1 tablespoon of oil to a wok over a medium heat and fry the ginger for 1 minute until fragrant. Next add the garlic, chillies/chiles and curry leaves. Fry for another 30 seconds until the garlic is golden.

Add the squid to the wok and stir-fry quickly for about 10 seconds. Serve immediately.

In China, turnip cake is made in big batches, brought round on a trolley and fried at the dinner table until caramelized and golden. Omit the sausage for a pescatarian version of the dish.

Turnip cake

1 Chinese turnip, pumpkin or carrot, peeled and grated
2 tablespoons sunflower oil
50 g/2 oz. raw prawns/shrimp, peeled, deveined and coarsely chopped
5 shiitake mushrooms, sliced
1 Chinese sausage, sliced
1 spring onion/scallion, sliced

127g/1 cup rice flour
1 tablespoon cornflour/cornstarch
1 teaspoon salt
1 teaspoon superfine/caster sugar
1 teapoon ground white pepper
2 tablespoons sunflower oil

Dipping sauce
2 tablespoons oyster sauce
1 tablespoon sesame oil

450-g/1-lb. loaf pan, lined with parchment paper

a large steamer

MAKES 1 LOAF

Simmer the grated turnip in 250 ml/1 cup water for 10 minutes until softened. Keep stirring while simmering and leave the pan uncovered so that the liquid gradually reduces by half. Set aside to cool.

Heat the oil in a large frying pan/skillet over medium heat. Add the chopped prawns/shrimp, mushrooms and sausage and stir-fry for 5 minutes. Stir in the chopped spring onion/scallion and fry for a minute longer. Let cool.

Combine the rice flour, cornflour/cornstarch, salt, sugar, and pepper in a large mixing bowl. Add the cooked turnips with their liquid and mix well. Lastly, stir in the cooked prawns/shrimp, mushrooms and sausage.

Pour the cake batter into the lined loaf pan. Place the pan into a steamer with plenty of water and steam over medium-high heat for 50 minutes. Cool the turnip cake for 10 minutes before removing from the loaf pan.

Use a sharp knife dipped in water to slice 3-cm/1-inch thick pieces. Add the oil to a non-stick cast iron pan/skillet over medium-low heat. Fry the cake slices on both sides until golden and crispy. Mix together the oyster sauce and sesame oil to form a dipping sauce and serve alongside the hot cake slices.

Vegetables

The fashionable clamshell shape of these buns shows off the vibrant colours of the vegetables. Take care with preparation as your knife skills will be on show. These buns are also good stuffed with the barbecue pork on page 15.

Chinese vegetable clamshell buns

1 batch Bread Dough, page 9
1 head of Chinese cabbage leaves
3 handfuls Chinese spinach
2 small leeks
1 carrot, peeled and grated
8 oyster mushrooms, sliced
3 Chinese chive stalks, white parts removed, sliced
2 tablespoons sunflower oil, plus extra for oiling the dough
a large handful of fresh coriander/cilantro, finely chopped
vegetarian stir-fry sauce, to serve

a bamboo steamer, lined with parchment paper

MAKES 16

Prepare, rise and roll out the bread dough following the instructions in the basic recipe on page 9.

Divide the dough into 16 round balls and flatten each slightly with a rolling pin into an oval shape, around 12 x 6 cm/4 ½ x 2 ⅓ inches. Cut parchment paper into 16 squares, each 12 cm/4 ½ inches. Use your fingers to lightly oil the surface of a piece of dough, place a square of paper on top and fold the dough in half so that the paper is in the centre. Cut another 16 squares of parchment paper just larger than the buns. Lay the paper squares on a tray and lightly dust with flour. Place a bun on top of each square on its side, cover with oiled clingfilm/plastic wrap and leave to rise for 30–40 minutes.

While the buns are rising, slice the cabbage leaves, spinach and leeks lengthwise into ribbons approximately 6 cm/2¼ inches long and 2 cm/¾ inch thick. Set aside.

Brush the top of each risen bun lightly with sunflower oil. Lift the buns on their squares and place in the bamboo steamer about 4 cm/1½ inches apart. Steam over boiling water for 15–20 minutes until light and fluffy.

Heat the sunflower oil in a wok and stir-fry all the vegetables and herbs for around 2–3 minutes. Add vegetarian stir-fry sauce to taste and give the vegetables a quick toss.

When the buns are ready, remove the parchment paper from the middle of each one and fill with the hot vegetables. Serve.

Vegetables take centre-stage in these warming and golden pumpkin and leek parcels. The interior of the dumpling should be soft in texture, flavoured beautifully with Chinese chives, ginger and Sichuan pepper. The egg dough provides just a little bite.

Pumpkin and leek dumplings

1 batch Egg Dough, page 8
100 g/3½ oz. firm tofu, drained and sliced into small cubes
a pinch of salt
40 g/¼ cup steamed pumpkin
1 leek, finely chopped
2 Chinese chive stalks, white parts removed, finely chopped
a handful of fresh coriander/ cilantro, chopped
1 teaspoon minced fresh ginger
2 Chinese cabbage leaves, finely chopped
1 teaspoon Sichuan pepper
1 teaspoon black pepper
2 tablespoons vegetarian stir-fry sauce
2 tablespoons sesame oil
black vinegar, for dipping

MAKES 16

Prepare the egg dough following the instructions in the basic recipe on page 8. While the dough is resting, make the filling. Lightly salt the tofu slices and set them aside for 30 minutes, before squeezing out the excess water.

In a large bowl, mix together the steamed pumpkin with the tofu, chopped vegetables, coriander/cilantro, ginger, Sichuan pepper, black pepper, vegetarian stir-fry sauce and sesame oil. Chill in the fridge for 30 minutes.

Roll out the egg dough, continuing to follow the instructions on page 8. Put a large teaspoon of filling into the centre of each skin. Dab a little water on one edge of the skin, fold in half over the filling and pinch the corners together to seal. Fold small pleats to seal up the middle. Continue with the rest of the batch, leaving the prepared dumplings on a tray lightly dusted with flour and covered with a damp kitchen cloth as you work.

Put a large pan of water on to boil. Lower the dumplings into the boiling water and cover with a lid. As soon as they start to float, they are cooked. Serve hot with black vinegar for dipping.

Alternatively, you can lightly pan-fry the uncooked dumplings and finish off the cooking by poaching the dumplings in a little stock or water (see page 11).

1 batch Wheat Dough, page 8

200 g/7 oz. firm tofu, drained and
  sliced into small cubes

a pinch of salt

1 leek, thinly sliced

60 g/½ cup sundried tomatoes,
  finely chopped

50 g/scant ½ cup black pitted
  olives, finely chopped

2 button mushrooms, finely
  chopped

2 Chinese chive stalks, white parts
  removed and finely chopped

a handful of fresh Chinese parsley,
  finely chopped

1 teaspoon Sichuan pepper

1 teaspoon freshly ground black
  pepper

2 tablespoons vegetarian stir-fry
  sauce

2 tablespoons sesame oil

Dipping sauce

1 tablespoon aged balsamic
  vinegar

2 tablespoons olive oil

a red shallot, finely chopped

a handful of fresh basil leaves,
  finely chopped

MAKES 16

Sun-kissed mediterranean ingredients fill this stylish little dumpling, resulting in a delicious clash of cultures. The strong tang of sundried tomatoes and olives are cooled by the mellow tofu. Pan-frying to get a crispy bottom is a nice finishing touch.

Tofu, sundried tomato and olive dumplings

Sprinkle a little salt over the tofu slices and set them aside for 30 minutes before squeezing out the excess water.

Prepare the wheat dough following the instructions from the basic recipe on page 8. While the dough is resting, prepare the filling.

In a bowl combine the tofu with the chopped vegetables, parsley, seasonings, vegetarian stir-fry sauce and sesame oil. Mix well and place in the fridge for 30 minutes to chill.

Roll out the skins, continuing to follow the recipe on page 8. Put a large teaspoon of filling into the centre of a skin. Dip your fingertips in a small dish of water and slightly moisten the edge of half the skin. Fold in half and pinch the edges together to form a simple crescent shape. Fold the two ends of the dumpling together and overlap to create a Chinese ingot shape. Seal with another dab of water if needed. Repeat until all the mixture and skins have been used.

Gently lower the dumplings into a pan of boiling water and cover with a lid. As soon as the dumplings start to float they should be ready. Alternatively, you can lightly pan-fry the boiled dumplings to make the bottoms crispy and golden.

To make the dipping sauce, mix the ingredients together in a small bowl. Serve the dumplings hot with the dipping sauce on the side.

Button, shiitake and oyster mushrooms are what I choose to fill these dumplings with, but you don't have to stick to this mixture exactly. The shiitake mushrooms bring a nice umami-like depth of flavour, so do use these if you can.

Assorted mushroom dumplings

1 batch Puff Pastry Dough, page 8
2 shallots, chopped
1 garlic clove, chopped
1 teaspoon minced fresh ginger
4 button mushrooms, sliced
4 shiitake mushrooms, sliced
4 oyster mushrooms, sliced
2 spring onions/scallions, sliced
salt and freshly ground black
    pepper
1 egg, beaten
black sesame seeds, to garnish

a large baking sheet, greased

MAKES 12

Prepare the water and butter doughs following the instructions in the basic recipe on page 8. Wrap the combined pastry balls in clingfilm/plastic wrap and rest in the fridge until needed.

Preheat the oven to 200°C/400°F/Gas 6.

In a small frying pan/skillet, cook the shallots over a medium heat for a few minutes until fragrant. Add the garlic and ginger and stir-fry together for a couple of minutes. Add the sliced mushrooms, spring onions/scallions and some salt and pepper. Fry until the mushrooms are cooked and the mixture is dry. Set aside to cool.

Roll each pastry ball into a rectangle 10 x 6 cm/4 x 2½ inches. Put a small tablespoon of filling on one side of a skin, brush the edges with beaten egg and fold in half to enclose the filling. Use a fork to make indentations and tightly seal the edges. Repeat with the rest of the dough and filling.

Place the parcels on the greased baking sheet, brush the tops with beaten egg and sprinkle with black sesame seeds to garnish. Bake in the preheated oven for 20–25 minutes or until golden brown. Serve warm.

Making noodles from scratch is rewarding and actually relatively easy. Add marinated tofu to bulk out if desired.

Vegetarian egg noodles

1 batch Egg Dough, page 8,
   plus extra flour for dusting
1 tablespoon groundnut oil
1 garlic clove, chopped
1 teaspoon minced fresh ginger
1 large red (bell) pepper, chopped
1 carrot, peeled and thinly sliced
vegetarian stir-fry sauce, to taste
60 g/1 cup beansprouts

2 heads pak choi/bok choy, sliced
1 red chilli/chile, chopped

Garnishes
chopped fresh coriander/cilantro,
chopped spring onion/scallion
sliced red chillies/chiles

SERVES 4

Prepare the egg dough following the instructions in the basic recipe on page 8. Leave to rest for 30 minutes in the fridge wrapped in clingfilm/plastic wrap.

Lightly dust the countertop with flour and roll out the dough into one big thin rectangle. Using a sharp knife, cut the dough into 1 cm/⅓ inch thin strips. Lightly dust the noodles with a little more flour to prevent them from sticking together.

Cook the noodles in a pan of boiling water until tender, around 3 minutes. Drain and cool the noodles in ice-cold water to rinse off the starch. Set aside while you prepare the vegetables.

Add the groundnut oil to a wok and gently cook the garlic and ginger until fragrant. Add the (bell) pepper and carrot and lightly fry for a further few minutes before adding the noodles.

Flavour the noodles with the vegetarian stir-fry sauce. Lastly, add the beansprouts, pak choi/bok choy and chilli/chile. Serve the dish straight away with the garnishes and extra stir-fry sauce to taste.

80 g/1¼ cup vermicelli rice
   noodles
14 edible rice papers
14 Bibb or other soft lettuce leaves
100 g/1¾ cups beansprouts
14 thin peeled carrot batons
14 thin cucumber batons
2 handfuls fresh coriander/cilantro
   leaves, roughly chopped
14 fresh mint leaves, roughly
   chopped
1 red chilli/chile, sliced

Dipping sauce
4 tablespoons hoisin sauce
4 tablespoons peanut butter
lime juice to taste

MAKES 14

Light and fresh, rice papers make a good gluten-free option for wheat-intolerant dim sum lovers. The peanut butter, hoisin and lime juice dipping sauce adds a touch of richness and piquancy to the dish, for those who want it.

Vietnamese vegetable summer rolls

Prepare the dipping sauce by mixing together all the ingredients in a small bowl. Cover and refrigerate until needed.

Cook the vermicelli according to instructions on the packet. Drain and set aside.

Soften the rice papers. Fill a large bowl with warm water. Carefully and slowly dip the rice papers in one by one. Leave each one for about 20 seconds until totally soft. Lay the rice papers out on a dry cloth as you finish.

On top of each rice paper, arrange a lettuce leaf (trimmed to size if needed) a small handful of vermicelli and a small handful of beansprouts. Add carrot, cucumber, herbs and chilli/chile, always keeping about 5 cm/2 inches of wrapper uncovered on each side of the filling.

Fold the uncovered sides inwards, then tightly roll the rice paper into a sausage shape around the filling. Repeat with the remaining ingredients.

Serve the rolls chilled with the dipping sauce to accompany.

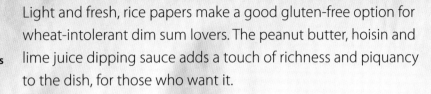

The Chinese take on a custard-filled doughnut is absolutely delicious, as one might expect. Perfect served in the afternoon with green tea to balance out the sweetness, or post-dinner party as the pièce de résistance.

Fried egg custard buns

1 batch Bread Dough, page 9
1½ tablespoons custard powder
75 g/½ cup wheat starch plus 2
    tablespoons plain/all-purpose
    flour
65 g/⅓ cup caster/granulated
    sugar
100 ml/⅓ cup milk
1 large egg plus another yolk,
    lightly beaten
2 tablespoons unsalted butter
sunflower oil for deep-frying

MAKES 16

Prepare the bread dough following the instructions in the basic recipe on page 9. While the dough is rising, prepare the custard filling.

Mix together the custard powder, wheat starch, flour and sugar in a small pan. Heat over a low heat and stir in the milk. Next slowly mix in the beaten egg. Add the butter and continue heating and stirring until well combined.

Remove the pan from the heat and turn the filling over and over with a wooden spoon or spatula until it forms a smooth ball and everything is well incorporated. Once cool place in the fridge to chill for at least 1 hour. Roll out 16 custard balls from the chilled custard.

After the bread dough has risen for the first time, divide and roll into 16 round balls. Roll out each ball into a circle (8 cm/3 inches in diameter) making the edges thinner than the centre.

Place a custard ball in the middle of a bread dough wrapper and then wrap it up completely inside the dough, pressing and smoothing over the join to seal. Keep the seal at the bottom and shape the bun round with palm of your hand. Repeat the process to finish all the buns. Cover with oiled clingfilm/plastic wrap and leave the buns in a warm place to rise for 30–40 minutes.

Heat the oil in a deep-fryer or large pan until it reaches 180°C/350°F. Lightly fry each custard bun until it turns golden brown and floats to the surface of the oil. Remove with a slotted spoon, drain on paper towels and serve hot.

Sweet

These pastries were introduced to Hong Kong teahouses in the 1940s and have since become a staple in Chinese bakeries. They differ from the European version in the unique way the puff pastry is made. The custard is passed through a sieve/strainer twice to ensure that it is smooth as silk.

Hong Kong egg tart

1 batch Puff Pastry Dough, page 8
100 g/⅓ cup fresh milk
50 g/¼ cup caster/superfine sugar
2 eggs
seeds from 1 vanilla pod/bean

a round fluted pastry cutter
12 individual mini tart pans

MAKES 12

Prepare the puff pastry dough following the instructions in the basic recipe on page 8. Whilst the dough is chilling make the filling.

Preheat the oven to 200°C/400°F/Gas 6.

Whisk together the milk, sugar, eggs and vanilla seeds in a large bowl until the sugar has fully dissolved. Pass the mixture twice through a sieve/strainer to make sure it is as smooth as possible.

Roll out each chilled dough ball and use a round cutter with a fluted edge to stamp out circles of dough to fit the mini tart pans. Lay a circle of dough in the tart pan and prick the base with a fork. Repeat for all 12 dough balls. Leave the tart pans to chill in the fridge for 5 minutes.

Pour the egg mixture into the tart shells to come ¾ of the way up the sides and bake in the preheated oven for 10 minutes. Lower the oven temperature to 170°C/325°F/Gas 3 and bake for a further 10 minutes. Leave to cool on a wire rack before serving.

Index